Lazlo Llama
Happiness Handbook

Stories From the Dali Llama's
Neighbor's Third Cousin

Written and Illustatrated by
Lazlo Llama

"In the service of others we let go of fear and welcome happiness."

-Lazlo Llama

© 2017, Red Circle Creative, LLC
Thanks for the Pizza

Stories

The Monkeys and the Golden Banana

The Llamas and the Chocolate

The Fallen Tree

The Grain of Sand

The Horse and the River

A Tower of Rocks

The Gnus

Listen Like the Moon

The Clock

A Pocket Full of Pebbles

The Mountain and the Sky

The Robin and the Cherry Tree

The Herons

The Llama and the Cat

The Cricket and the Fawn

Reflections of Ewe

The Key to Happiness

The Monkeys and the Golden Banana

Deep in the verdant jungle, lived a group of playful monkeys. They loved to swing through the vast green landscape, playing together while they searched for food.

One rainy afternoon, the chattering monkeys discovered a strange object. Their eyes widened with amazement as it glistened in the sunlight. Nestled between two gum trees lay a golden banana!

All at once, each monkey wanted the treasure for themselves. "I'm the most beautiful!" boasted one monkey, as she lunged to take the gilded fruit. "But I'm the fastest!" said another monkey, snatching the banana first. "I'm the strongest!" bellowed a large monkey, yanking it away.

The troop began fighting over who should have it. They yelled and pulled each other's hair while grabbing for the golden banana.

Suddenly, the banana slipped out of one monkey's hand and flew high into the air. They all watched, as the shiney bobble tumbled down a raveen, into a fast moving river. Sploosh! The monkeys stopped bickering and looked at each other...and they started laughing.

"How silly to fight over something you can't even eat!" they thought. As the rains washed the jungle leaves, the monkeys began to play again.

They lived the rest of their days in peace.

The farther you are from your stuff,
the closer you are to happiness.

−Lazlo Llama

The Llamas and the Chocolate

A small pack of llamas found a paper bag filled with chocolate left on the side of the road by a traveler. The curious llamas peeked inside the bag and discovered one piece of chcolate for each of them.

With a crinkle, the excited llama stuck his head in and ate his right away.

Next, the thrifty llama carefully pulled her piece out and gently set it in a shady place to save for later.

The forgetfull llama, lost in watching the clouds, realized it was his turn. He rummaged in the bag for what seemed like hours, but eventually he pulled out a piece. Unfortunately, he left it in the sun and it melted.

Finally, the purple llama, after some wiggling and getting the bag stuck on her nose, extracted the final piece. She sat, wondering what she could do with her chcolate to help her savor it forever.

Then she noticed a marmot sitting all alone on a hill who looked hungry.

She gave it to him.

Remember llamas...
if you can share your chocolate,
you can share anything.

—Lazlo Llama

The Fallen Tree

High in the mountains, on a stormy night, a forest of cedar trees swayed in the dark. The Wind shouted loudly and forced its swollen hands through the timber. Wind's cousin, Lightining, struck the mountain repleatedly and all the cedar held their roots tightly in fear.

Suddenly, Lightining struck one cedar tree - Crack-a-lacka! - and she fell with a great heaving noise.

For many days the cedar lay on the ground, sad, worried and afraid. "What will become of me?", she thought.

Gradually, the rains gave her a soft bed to rest on. Then, a chorus of frogs happened upon her, and graciously asked if they could make their home inside her cozy hollow. "Of course!", she entreated. They hopped in, tickling her bark.

A family of racoons, also in need of shelter, made their home under her shady tunk, and she welcomed them too. She stretched her back wide as a place for hikers to rest and bear cubs to jostle. When children came to the forest to play, they would use her as a bridge to imaginary places, and claim her for hide and seek, filling the cedar with their laughter.

She felt joy.

One night the Wind returned, pulling its way through the forest and snapping branches as it went. As the other trees held their roots in fear, the fallen cedar lay unafraid. The Wind could do nothing to her now.

She slept peacefully, surrounded by her friends, giving them safety in her cavernous heart.

> In the service of others, we let go of fear, and welcome happiness.
>
> —Lazlo Llama

The Grain of Sand

One day, a tiny grain of sand asked a larger grain of sand, "What is my purpose?" The large grain smiled a warm smile and looked down at the little grain of sand, with all of its hope. "You reflect light into the world."

The small flickering silica pondered for a moment, then said, "I am so small, I can only shine so much. "True," agreed the large grain, bathed in the warmth of the sun. Then the larger grain of sand smiled and put its arm around the tiny grain of sand and added,

"...but when billions of us shine together, this beach looks bright from space."

The Horse and the River

A Horse stood at the edge of a wild river starring at a lovely field of tall grass on the other side. "If I wait for just the right moment," thought the Horse. But the water swirled and rushed with no sign of stopping. Affraid of washing away in the strong current, the Horse changed her mind, "Maybe if I find just the right spot."

She moved down the river to a bamboo thicket and peeked in. While the shallow water stood still among the reeds, beyond that, the dark pool looked too deep. Sure to drown if she tried that spot, she walked on.

Next she came to a rocky shole. The water slowed down and bubbled over the pebbles, but only for a little, then it picked up speed and dashed into large boulders! Not wanting to break her leg in the rapids, the Horse continued upstream. Then, in the distance, the Horse saw a bridge.

So she used that.

Even the wildest river has a way across. It's usually a bridge.

-Lazlo Llama

A Tower of Rocks

A strong Lion worked hard to build a tower of rocks so its family could see the tower for miles and never lose their home. First, a strong base of huge rocks, then flat rocks, then rocks that shine in the sun. Day after day, the Lion searched for the perfect rock to make the next layer of the tower. "Come and play," the Lion's cubs would ask, but the Lion knew there was only so much time to finish the tower. The Lion diligently placed stone after stone. The Lion's cubs watched the Lion focus on the Tower with ferocious intensity.

One day, after the Lion pushed a particularly huge boulder up the hill, the cubs asked the Lion, "Is the Tower more important than us?" The Lion stopped.

Starring at the Tower shadowed against the sunset, the Lion picked up the cubs in its arms and laughed, "Nothing is more important than you!" To this day the Tower remains unfished on the hill, but that's okay.

It was only a tower of rocks.

> If your desire to work exceeds your capacity to love, you might want to take a break.
>
> —Lazlo Llama

The Gnus

There was once a gnu who loved to paint. He lived on a hill above his village. Every day the fox would come and tell him about what was happening in town. The fox, a gifted story teller, loved to embelish and tell wild tales of predators ransaking the village, and terrible floods, and worst of all, pizza shortages.

The gnu awoke every morning, anxious for the fox's words to the exclusion of his other endeavours. The gnu stopped painting. He found he could only draw the horrors of the fox's stories, and his brush felt too heavy to lift. Scared to go outside, the gnu began to take less walks in the woods, and take in less the wonders of the sky.

One day the fox came and told the gnu the village had been burned to the ground. Having not seen the smoke from his window, the gnu questioned the fox, "Are you sure the village is gone?" "Oh yes. In a fireball of splinters and ash." The gnu thought for a moment. Then he opened his door and ran to the village, only to find that it was still there. A fire in the night had burned a bail of hay, and one marmot was hurt. The gnu offered to help, and gave the marmot a clean cloth from his art bag to use as a fresh bandage. From that day, the gnu vowed never to listen to the fox again, and he moved into town and opened an art gallery.

The fox still talks, but no one really listens.

Listen Like the Moon

A troubled raccoon climbed to the top of a house and sat, looking up at the sky. The Moon greeted her with a warm smile. The raccoon could no longer control herself and blurted out, "It's so unfair!" She explained to the moon how the other raccoons steal her best foraging spots, and don't help to find more. The Moon listened quietly, not juding, not trying to solve her problem. The raccoon felt better and they enjoyed the rest of the night, lost in the stars.

The next night, a panda, wandered through the grassland crying because one of his friends had wrecked his bamboo fort. He complained to the Moon, who spilled her gentle light onto the panda's tears. The panda felt the comfort of the Moon's reserved understanding.

Another night, a confused cheetah asked the Moon whom to marry. The Moon smiled and let the cheetah weigh the merits of each, and the merits of not marrying at all, while gently accepting everything the cheetah had to say. The cheetah made up its own mind and thanked the Moon for her counsel.

On yet another night, an eagle soared to the top of a tree and asked the Moon what he should do. The Wind destroyed his nest. Should he rebuild it? Should he move to another tree? The vexed eagle left his pain at the Moon's feet. The Moon bathed him with a hug of her cream light and her shining face comforted the eagle. The eagle knew just what to do.

Then one day, a giraffe who couldn't sleep, stood starring at the Moon. She explained how her mind filled with thoughts, and she never felt relaxed enough to dream. The Moon understood. With a gentle nod she listed to the giraffe. After a few hours, the giraffe felt unburdened and sleepy. Before nodding off, the giraffe looked at the happy face of the silent Moon and asked, "How did you get to be such a good listener?" The Moon winked and replied,

"Lot's of practice."

When I'm meditating, people think I'm listening.

Win, win.

—Lazlo Llama

The Clock

High above a bustling zebra village stood a collosal clock. Amidst the constant hustle of hooves, a small zebra looked up and marveled at how everyone ran their lives according to its massive hands. "Who made the clock?" the little zebra asked a passing black and white blur. "Someone, long, long ago," blurted a zebra zipping to have her mane trimmed. "Why do we follow the clock?" the little zebra continued. "If we don't, there'd be chaos!" the long maned mare yelled back as she hurried away.

Life in the buzzing village hummed along, until one day, a horrible pinging noise echoed from inside the giant clock. Sproing!

The entire town came to a stand still. The zerbras looked up and noticed in disbelief that the hands of the ancient time piece stood perfectly still. A little scared and unsure, they all slowly resumed their daily routines.

Gradually, the zebras grew less busy, afraid to pack their day full of so many tasks it might overflow. The zerbras walked instead of ran. Without the constant overbearing clock, they had no excuse to be rude. They began to have long conversations, and look up at the sky, and get lost in thought. The village became a slower place.

After many years, on a calm, cool, cloudless day, a little zebra looked up at the clock in wonder. "Who made the clock?" the little zebra asked a group gathered on a hill. "Someone, long, long ago," explained a zebra, enjoying herself in the light of the sun. "Why don't we fix the clock?" the little zebra continued. The mare smiled at the little zebra and said,

"If we did, there'd be chaos."

There's nothing more peaceful than a llama with a broken watch.

-Lazlo Llama

A Pocket Full of Pebbles

A badger kept a small pocket in his fur for pebbles. Every time he did something he regretted, he'd pick up a small pebble and deposit it in his pocket to remind him of his shame and not to do it again.

When he told a lie to protect his feelings, he'd find a smooth stone and slip it in. If he grew harsh with a friend over a piece of tree bark, he'd apologize and add another piece of gravel. After a while, the pocket began to buldge. It kept him from getting hugs from the other badgers. Eventually, the pocket became so heavy he could not skip, or play or run.

One day he tried to cross a swollen river, but the pocket weighed him down so much he could not swim. Fighting for his life against the current, he emptied the pebbles from his pocket and they fell, disappearing into the murky water to the bottom of the river. Gasping for air, he climbed on to the bank safely. For the first time in many years, he felt light and unburdened. The sky seemed closer, and the ground squished warmly under his feet. Delighted, he skipped all the way home.

He left the pebbles at the bottom of the river where they belong.

I don't hold on to my regrets...

because llamas don't like to carry stuff we don't have to.

-Lazlo Llama

The Mountain and the Sky

The wonderous sky, stretched out above all things; ever moving and changing. The steadfast mountain, lived a constant life, rooted to the Earth; ever stoic and sure. Every day the sky would change color, from black to midnight blue, then pink, orange, light aqua and back again. Clouds would form on the sky's face, and rain would fall, or sometimes it appeared crystal azure like a shallow beach. But no matter how hard the sky tried, it could never be as constant as the mountain. It could never hold fast to one color, or know what came next.

Meanwhile, the mountain spent its days firm on a foundation, unwavering, no matter the circumstance. Regardless of weather, or temperature, sun or darkness, the mountain stood quietly, dependable amidst it all. No matter how the mountain tried, it could never flow free like the sky. It could never move, or flush pink or stretch beyond its place.

One day, the mountain and the sky met, as they had thousands of times before. Each greeted the day, but this time, as they touched, joy overcame them. They finally realized...

sometimes you're a mountain, sometimes you're the sky. It takes both to make the world.

The Robin and the Cherry Tree

A red-breasted robin loved to fly with her friends over a cherry orchard. One day, they landed on a cherry tree and her friends all dared each other to try the sweet fruit. "Anyone who doesn't try it is a chicken!" taunted one of the birds. Robin's aren't chickens, so the robin bit into a big juicy cherry. She had never tasted anything like it. The sweet, juicy inside bristled her feathers. They all left the orchard, laughing and singing.

The next day the robin wanted another cherry, and so she went back alone. This time she had two. Then the next day three. Then four. Soon, she could think of nothing but the next cherry feast. When her friends talked, her mind would wonder back to the orchard. She stopped playing with other robins and spent all her time finding more and more delectable cherries.

One cloudy day, sick from over indulging, she promised herself that she wouldn't eat anymore. But the next day, despite her promise, she went to the orchard again. She couldn't stop. She sat beneath the trees worried and alone. Suddenly, she heard a noise that sounded like whimpering from behind another tree. She slowly approached the sound and discovered a finch with a broken wing huddled up against the bark of an alder tree. The robin offered to help, and she put the finch on her back and carried her home. The finch family greeted their brother with gladness, and offered the robin supper. She accepted and they shared stories late into the night.

The following day on her way back to the orchard, the robin happened upon a toad who had fallen in a hole too deep to jump out. Not one to leave another animal to suffer, the robin offered to help, "I can drop sticks in the hole, then you can climb up and jump out." "Oh yes, that would help so much!" smiled the toad, and the robin fetched stick after stick until the toad hopped free. The toad graciously thanked the robin, and they enjoyed each other's company for the rest of the day.

The day after that, the robin awoke as the sun gently crossed her face. For the first time in a long time, her mind filled with memories of the finch and toad, and not the orchard. The robin decided to help another animal that day, then two the next, then three, the four. For the rest of her days, the more time she spent in the service of other animals, the less she cared about cherries.

Many years later, the old robin went back to the orchard. She found the tree where she had taken her first bite of cherry, and there beneath it sat a young robin. He had indulged in a cherry feast and couldn't fly. The old robin gently sat beside him, smiled and said,

"Here, let me show you the way."

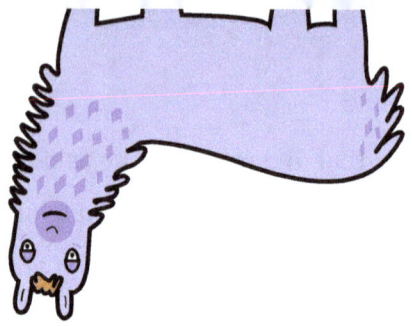

If two lost llamas can't find their way, at least they can keep each other company.

-Lazlo Llama

The Herons

Two white winged herons flew high above a valley. Feeling the breeze in their wings, they swooped down toward the riverbed below. In the forest, the herons came upon a squirrel sitting on a massive pile of nuts. "Ya better not take any of my nuts!" shouted the squirrel, as he spread his hands out wide. Then he started to pull on a giant leaf sled he created to carry them to his tree house. Nuts kept falling off the top of the pile, and the squirrel kept scolding the acorns. "Get back on there!" He struggled, and cursed.

Without a word, the older heron flew over and scooped up both the squirrel and his make shift nut transport, and flew them to the squirrel's tree. "Put me down! You are trying to steal my stuff!" The older haron smiled and gently set him down at home. "Good riddance!" yelled the squirrel, and he yanked the nuts inside.

The two herons resumed their flight over the forest. For hours the younger heron flew in silence saying nothing about what happened. Then suddenly, he blurted out, "That squirrel was so selfish and rude, yet you picked him up and helped him. How could you do that?" The older heron smiled and said,

"It must be hard for you to fly while still holding on to the squirrel. You should leave him by his tree as I did."

The Llama and the Cat

There once was a llama who thought a cat was talking to her. The cat said, "You can't beat me at chess, so don't even try."

Rude, right? For years, the llama kept practicing chess, in hopes the feline disparager would one day change his mind. No matter where the llama traveled, even as far as San Franscisco, the cat would sneak in from the alley as the llama setup her chess pieces to throw his taunt. "You haven't thought of everything," he would hiss. One day, after hours and hours of planning her moves, the llama shook her fur vigourously and came to a startling realization.

Cat's dont talk...and she's awesome at chess.

When the demons of self-doubt start whispering in your ear, remember...

There's no such thing as demon's dude, you got this.

-Lazlo Llama

The Cricket and the Fawn

One afternoon an auburn fawn grazed in a field of tall grass surrounded by colorful flowers. She chatted with a cricket while she munched, "I'm not as tall as the other fawns, nor as coordinated." The cricket sat, listening to her crunch and explain while enjoying a breeze. The fawn continued, "I also saw the orangutans house, and boy, is it nice. It's covered in leaves, and grass. I have to live in a field. Plus, have you seen the faces of the lionesses, they are so beautiful."

The cricket looked up at the fawn with a smile, "That depends," he postulated. "Depends? Depends on what?" the fawn doubted. "How fast can you run?" questioned the wise bug. "Not very fast," confessed the fawn. "How fast can you run compared to a snail?" "I'm much faster than a snail," smiled the fawn. "And how fast can you run compared to the cheetah?" asked the cricket. "I'm much slower than a cheetah," the fawn said, hanging her head. "You see," explained the little green sage,

"Compared to the snail you are fast, compared to the cheetah you are slow, but compared to you, you are just right."

Reflections of Ewe

A young ewe drank every morning at a still pool in a shady glen. As she took a sip, she would look down at her reflection and chat with it. "I don't think the other sheep like us very much," her reflection would snarl. "I hadn't really noticed," offered the ewe. "They think we look baaad," proposed her silvery shadow. "You don't know that for sure," the ewe countered, "I like us."

On they argued, about many issues. Who their friends were, what the other sheep really meant when they said something, what they should do that day, what order to do them in. Eventually the ewe realized that her reflection seemed angry, petty and negative most of the time.

One sunny afternoon, the ewe summoned her courage and asked her reflection, "You seem pessimistic most of the time, my friend. Why is that?" "It's my job to see the worst side of things, so that you realize they are there," her reflection replied. "But things in my life aren't as bad as you make them out to be. It doesn't help since it's not true," explained the ewe. Her visage stood still, not knowing what to say.

From then on, the ewe drank from a waterfall.

The Key to Happiness

A wise long-haired baboon sat in front of a large stone door, looking out at the sunset. A young ferret scurried up to it and asked, "I heard happiness hides behind that door, but I don't have the key, will you share it with me?" The primate smiled a knowing smile and said, "Gladly, but I put the key down in the forest years ago. I will tell you where to look for it." Excited, the ferret perked up its ears and listened. "I set the key under the bed of the a muskrat in the valley," explained the guardian. Without another word, the ferret zoomed away.

After a short journey, the ferret knocked on the muskrat's door only to find that she was ill. The ferret offered to gather ingredients for soup to help her feel better, then cleaned the house because the muskrat could not move well. After cooking and helping her tidy, the ferret asked for the key. "I don't believe I have a key, but you can check," shrugged the muskrat. The ferret looked under the bed, then all over, but could not find the key. Frustrated, the ferret stomped back to the baboon.

"You lied to me!" shouted the ferret. "There was no key under her bed." "No?" asked the wise monkey, "Hmmm. I made a mistake, pardon me. Yes, yes, I remember the last place I had the key. I stored it in a small cave under the waterfall. Here, take this mango with you for the journey." The ferret hurried off, excited to finally have the key. She came to the waterfall, but before the ferret could go behind the shimmering curtain, she heard a voice, grumbling. Next to the waterfall sat a rat, who hadn't eaten for days. Never to let another animal go hungry, the ferret shared the mango with him. They sat and talked about sharing, and how it made them feel. There was enough for everyone. After a delightful conversation, the ferret used a palm leaf to divert the cascading water and searched the cave...but there was no key. Disappointed, the ferret trudged back to the babboon.

"The key wasn't there either. When will I find the key? I'm afraid I will never find it," worried the ferret. "Please forgive my mistake," the sage replied. "I am old and forgetful. I remember now. I set the key down at the top of that mountain, next to a flat rock," the ancient mammal said, pointing. "When you get there, wait until the sun goes down, then the moon will show you the location." The ferret looked hopefully at the tall, mist-shrouded edifice, and sped off.

After climbing the rocky cliffs to the top, the squirrel looked out at the breadth of the valley below. In awe, she sat on the flat rock and watched the sun retreat slowly. She began to let go of her fear of never finding the key. She thought of cleaning up for the muskrat and sharing with the rat. She realized that whatever happened, the world would go on, and she felt her place in it. She meditated for what seemed like hours.

Finally, when the sun retreated and the moon came, the ferret asked about the key. She searched the mountain top in the moonlight. Again, the key did not appear. The ferret thanked the moon and returned to the stone door, and the baboon.

"I searched each place you said. I feel at peace now, yet I never found the key," confessed the squirrel. Then, the baboon pushed on the door and it opened. Smiling, the baboon explained,

"You assumed the door was locked."

Cover Illustration Copyright © 2017 by Lazlo Llama
Cover design by Lazlo Llama
Book design by Lazlo Llama
Editing by Edwina Llama
Illustrations © 2017 Lazlo Llama
Stories and quotes by © 2017 Lazlo Llama

www.ingramcontent.com/pod-product-compliance
Lightning Source LLC
Chambersburg PA
CBHW050547300426
44113CB00012B/2295